D1569504

Suffer from BURNOUT?

give 'em the F.I.N.G.E.R.!

A Guide for your Recovery

by Mark Yarbrough

Suffer from BURNOUT?

give 'em the F.I.N.G.E.R.!

A Guide for your Recovery

by Mark Yarbrough

Yarbook Publishing, LLC
Amherst, Texas
yarbookpublishing.com

Acknowledgments

To my proofreaders and editors: Scott Say, Laney Dickey, Eric Dickey, Shanna Friday, and especially my sister, Jill Tate – thank you for your tireless efforts. I have learned more about comma placement in the past few months than I ever learned in school!

To my cousin, J. Dennis Smith with Paper Graphics and Printing, and Dennis Blair with Visual Basics, thank you for the book cover design.

To my son, Alex, thanks for all your help with the book cover, websites, and supplying me with a plethora of other information.

I would especially like to thank my wife, Jerry, and my entire family, who have always been there for me. They have always encouraged me and my dreams, no matter how crazy they might be (my dreams, not my family).

Thank you readers for putting your time and energy into this book. If you believe you are suffering from BURNOUT, know that you are not alone. Also, know that I truly believe my F.I.N.G.E.R. philosophy will help.

-Mark-

Dedication

This book is dedicated in memory of Ashley – the most wonderful, crazy, beautiful daughter that a dad could ever hope to have come into his life. I love you always, and will see you again in heaven.

- Dad

Contents

About the Author

Mark Yarbrough was born in Austin, Texas, and has resided in Texas his entire life. He and his wife Jerry were high school sweethearts, and have been married for over 28 years. They had two children, Alex and Ashley.

Mark attended undergraduate school at Abilene Christian University, earning his bachelor's degree in Finance. After graduating, Mark worked for Dallas Federal/Bright Banc Savings as a loan counselor, personal banker, and branch manager.

While raising a family, Mark then went to law school at Texas Tech School of Law. Upon his graduation, Mark went to work in his father's law office. Mark jokingly called the firm Yarbrough & Father.

In 1993, Mark was elected as the County & District Attorney of Lamb County, Texas. He has since been re-elected to serve a total of five terms, or 20 years. There, he has prosecuted sex offenders, capital murderers, and various other defendants.

Also in 1993, Mark was certified to teach the Walk Thru the Bible Old Testament seminars. In his spare time, Mark enjoys playing basketball and golf, and vacationing on the beaches of the Caribbean.

About the Title

Introduction

So, you read the title and your first question was, "Which Finger?"

Actually, you may have thought that I have some serious anger issues. Your first thought may have been, "Is he referring to 'flipping-off' somebody with the middle finger?" Do you show your middle finger to BURNOUT and really let it know how you feel? This could be the first book that really explores the medicinal benefit of hand gestures. Well, in case my mom reads this book, she and you should know that the book has nothing to do with the middle finger. No need for any *Lifebuoy* soap or willow tree branches for me. Thanks in large part to my parents, I don't know that I have ever "flipped-off" anyone.

Perhaps I was referring to your forefinger. Maybe this is more of a self-help book showing you how you are #1, and nobody can stop you. You are the center of the universe, and the universe is good. You point your forefinger at BURNOUT, and order it to go away. It's that simple. Well, as Marty the Moose told Chevy Chase in the movie *Vacation*: "Sorry Folks," this book is not about the forefinger either.

Better yet, maybe the "finger" referred to in the title is your ring finger. Maybe I take a more "lovey-dovey" look at stress and BURNOUT. After all, even the Captain & Tennille sang, "Love will keep us together." Even with things falling apart around you, love will keep you together. That sounds really sweet. I am already seeing butterflies and rainbows just thinking about it. Sadly, I am not romantic enough to write a book about the ring finger - just ask my wife!

What if the book is all about that little pinky finger? In the same way that a child or grandchild might have you wrapped around his little finger, you would learn how you could take your BURNOUT and just wrap your finger around it. Now, that would be a good read. As Lee Corso might say, "Not so fast my friend."

This book is not about any one particular finger. F.I.N.G.E.R. in the title is an acronym for my philosophy of life. F.I.N.G.E.R. outlines six checklist items for you to follow that will help you to cope with and/or to recover from BURNOUT.

> F is for fun.
> I is for important.
> N is for notes.
> G is for giving back.
> E is for escape.
> R is for remember.

Later in the book, I have devoted a chapter for each of the above six topics to discuss them in greater detail. I can tell you as a fellow BURNOUT sufferer, the F.I.N.G.E.R. philosophy has worked for me and I truly believe it will work for you as well.

So, I could have named the book "The F.I.N.G.E.R. Philosophy, an acronym of BURNOUT management." My mom would have been much happier with that title. But, let's be honest — a book with that title would not be in your hands right now. You have to admit, that the current title at least piqued your curiosity. Studies show that seventy-two percent of potential customers buy a book based solely on the book title. Okay, I made up the previous statement. I have no idea how many people buy books based upon their titles. What matters to me is that you are reading this book, and for that I am very thankful.

I am the elected County & District Attorney for Lamb County, Texas. I have been so for almost 20 years, and I have practiced as an attorney for over 22 years. Prior to becoming an attorney, I worked in the banking industry for four years. I know what you are thinking – that you are going to get to read all kinds of interesting legal jargon. That I will astound you with *res ipsa locitur* and other big fancy words. Sorry to disappoint you, but that's just not me. I was raised in a small West Texas town, and all the schooling in the world couldn't get the hick out of me. Therefore, this book should be an easy read. It should also be a fun read.

My goal with the book is two-fold. First and foremost, I hope to share some ideas with you the reader that you might not have thought of in the past. I believe those ideas contained in my F.I.N.G.E.R. philosophy will lessen any hold that BURNOUT has on you and help in your recovery process. Lastly, I hope that by actually putting my thoughts into words that I too will benefit and continue to improve from my BURNOUT.

Thanks again.

-Mark-

Chapter 1

So, Just what is BURNOUT?

I love my beautiful wife Jerry to death, but she is notorious for thinking she is suffering from some mysterious ailment. Her head hurts and she has swine flu. She watches TV, sees a new disease, and is convinced she has contracted it. If you know someone like this, or if you are someone like this, you know what happens next. Next is the internet search for the symptoms of the disease. Invariably the symptoms involve some contact with a spider in the Amazon or contaminated Brussel sprouts. Trust me, my wife has not been to the Amazon and avoids Brussel sprouts like the plague. So, she realizes the symptoms do not match with hers, takes a deep breath, forgets all about it, and moves on with her life.

BURNOUT is the same way. You first have to know the symptoms in order to determine if you suffer from the condition. The medical condition known as "BURNOUT" was first used by Herbert Freudenberger in 1974. In the 1970s, Dr. Christina Maslach developed a measurement inventory that weighed the effects of emotional exhaustion and the reduced sense of personal accomplishment.[1] In the years following her study, psychologists have attempted to define the symptoms of BURNOUT. BURNOUT has been defined as a state of emotional, mental, and physical exhaustion caused by excessive and prolonged stress. Other studies have identified symptoms of BURNOUT as including: chronic fatigue, inappropriate anger at co-workers or family, self-criticism, irritability, cynicism, negativism, and a hair-trigger display of emotions.[2]

All those definitions and symptoms are fine, for psychologists. I don't know about you, but I need a more "down to earth" list of symptoms. Therefore, my non-expert checklist would include:

- ☐ Are you mad all the time?
- ☐ Are you tired all the time?
- ☐ Do you no longer care what happens at work or home?
- ☐ Do you just feel worn out?
- ☐ Is most of your day spent on things that you find mind-numbingly dull?
- ☐ Do you feel like nothing you do makes a difference?
- ☐ Do you feel like other people don't care what you think or do?
- ☐ Have you quit taking on responsibilities?
- ☐ Do you try to get away from people?
- ☐ Are you taking longer to get things done?
- ☐ Have you tried to cope by using things like food, alcohol, or drugs?
- ☐ Do you take things out on others?
- ☐ Are you in the habit of coming in late to work, leaving early, or just plain skipping it all together?

Most of us have days when we don't want to get out of bed. You hit the alarm more than once. You start thinking of excuses in your head about how to get out of going to work. You have used the excuse that your aunt died three times in the past month and your parents had no brothers or sisters. You don't want to deal with people that day, whether they are customers, clients, or co-workers. You don't care about what is on tap for the work day and you know that nobody else that you work with cares about what you do either. The above scenario happens to all of us. All of us have bad days. BURNOUT is more than that.

One of my favorite children's books to read to my kids was *Alexander and the Terrible, Horrible, No Good, Very Bad Day* by Judith Viorst. Among other things, Alexander woke up with gum in his hair, didn't get a prize in the cereal box, didn't get a window seat on the way to school, had no dessert in his lunch, got pushed in the mud, had a cavity, had the elevator door shut on his foot, made a mess at his dad's office, had lima beans for supper, and there was kissing on TV. Now that's a bad day. BURNOUT feels like that, only instead of one bad day, it is like that every day.

BURNOUT is also more than just daily stress. You can recognize when you are experiencing stress, but you don't always notice BURNOUT when it happens. The symptoms of BURNOUT can take months to recognize. The chart on the following page illustrates the main differences between stress and BURNOUT.

Stress	BURNOUT
characterized by over engagement	characterized by disengagement
emotions are over reactive	emotions are blunted
produces urgency and hyperactivity	produces helplessness and hopelessness
exhausts physical energy	exhausts motivation, drive, ideals, and hope
leads to anxiety disorders	leads to detachment and depression
causes disintegration	causes demoralization
primary cause is physical	primary cause is emotional

Stress may kill you prematurely, and you won't have enough time to finish what you started. On the other hand, BURNOUT may never kill you, but your life may not seem worth living.[3] If you compared BURNOUT to the flu, then stress would be the diarrhea. It may not cure your BURNOUT to be rid of stress, but it sure would make you feel a lot better.

It is estimated that BURNOUT affects approximately 14.8 million adults in America. That is about 6.7% of the population over 18 years of age.[4]   According to the 1990 Johns Hopkins University study, the number one profession that suffers from BURNOUT is attorneys. That might sound like poetic justice to some of you, but being an attorney myself, it is a little scary. Attorneys are obviously susceptible to BURNOUT because of the nature of their positions. Attorneys often hear about the worst situations in people's lives. They hear about the problems of divorce, injuries in accidents, feuds with neighbors, and family disagreements in estates. Prosecutors are perhaps the attorneys in the most precarious position. Prosecutors deal with the worst of humanity – criminals who prey on little children, sexual assault cases, and murderers, just to name a few.

BURNOUT affects more women than men. No, I didn't say men cause BURNOUT for women. However, BURNOUT can be caused from daily stresses from marriage, children, or loss of a loved one. The most common contributor for BURNOUT is work.

One of the main problems associated with BURNOUT is the domino effect it has in a person's relationships. The expression "a few flakes working together can cause an avalanche of destruction," especially holds true for those that suffer from BURNOUT. BURNOUT victims often use their symptoms to treat others badly. Sometimes they are rude and sometimes those suffering from BURNOUT ignore those around them altogether. Then, the cycle continues. Those friends then start treating others around them poorly and, before you know it, everyone is worse off.

Now that you know the symptoms of BURNOUT, ask

yourself: Are you a potential BURNOUT victim? Was there a symptom listed in the chart above that made you relax and realize that you are okay? If so, thanks for buying the book; you can stop reading now. Just remember to recommend the book to your friends! Or, you could keep reading just for the fun of it. Or, maybe you know of someone else who meets the symptoms and you want to help them. If so, I hear the author really has some good chapters coming next.

In all seriousness, if the symptoms listed in the chart scared you or you thought "Hey, that describes me," then know that I really believe that the F.I.N.G.E.R. philosophy I discuss in this book will help.   Also know this --- those listed symptoms also described me to a tee.

In the next couple of chapters, I am going to tell you what happened in my life to make me suffer from BURNOUT. The remainder of the book will be devoted to my F.I.N.G.E.R. philosophy, which develops a way to cope and a way to overcome.

Chapter 2

Christmas 2004

I love Christmas. I love everything about it. I make Christmas candy, do all the shopping, decorating, and wrapping of presents. I know, I know, I am way too touch with my feminine side. I am fifty years old and Santa still comes to my house. Don't even get me started on the Christmas movies and television shows. Growing up, my brother Scot and I were always the Heat and Snow Misers. When Clark Griswold got that "jelly of the month" bonus, a tear almost came to my eye. I mean after all, it is the gift that keeps on giving. Of course I watch and love *Miracle on 34th Street*, *A Christmas Story*, and *It's a Wonderful Life*. But sadly, it is worse than that. I will also sit down with my wife and watch those *Hallmark* and *Lifetime* movies about Christmas. I just lost my man card, didn't I?

I am a Christian and I grew up attending a fairly conservative church. That church drilled it into our heads that Christmas was just another day on the calendar. It is true that the birth of Christ was not necessarily on the 25th of December, but I still love celebrating Christmas. Even though I might wish that people celebrated Christ more than just a few times a year, I still like it that HE is celebrated at all. It thrills me to see people coming together to donate to the less fortunate, to worship together, and, for lack of a better way to put it, let the Spirit guide them. All of the wonderful things listed above happen because society recognizes that Christmas is something that should be celebrated. And that is reason number thirty-seven why I love Christmas.

Christmas 2004 was no different. Our son Alex had returned home from his first semester at college. Our daughter Ashley was 16 ½ years old and a junior in high school. We woke up Christmas morning, and sure enough Santa had come and brought us all kinds of goodies. Alex's girlfriend (now wife) Kelsey came over that day and we all opened more gifts. We ate together, played together, and just enjoyed each other's company. It was that kind of family time where everything just comes together. Everything was right with the world.

We went to church on the 26th. On the 27th, we returned a few of our Christmas gifts. I returned a really bright tie that Ashley had gotten me for Christmas. Also on the 27th, we went to Ashley's basketball tournament.

Each year, our small community organizes a Christmas tournament during the week after Christmas. To have enough teams play in the tournament, our school not only enters the local varsity team but also the junior varsity team plays in the tournament. The varsity basketball coach had asked Ashley to play varsity, but she had chosen to stay on junior varsity and play with her friends and with her coach. Her goal that week was to try and win some games and to play the varsity, and beat them.

The evening of the 27th, Alex and Kelsey went out on a date. Ashley stayed home that night. We had gotten the game *MadGab* for Christmas, and my wife and I and Ashley played it that night. We had a great time laughing at each other trying to say the phrases in that game. Later that night, Ashley played the piano. She liked a song that we sang in church called *Listen to Our Hearts*, by Steven Curtis Chapman. She played that song.

On the 28th, all of us were up early, except for Alex. He was enjoying sleeping in during his college break. My wife left first for an early appointment at her work. Ashley was soon to follow. She had an early game that morning, and had to be at the gym 30 minutes before the game started. Although I had to go to work that morning, I was going to Ashley's game first. I remember telling Ashley to block out for rebounds, because the team she was playing was pretty aggressive. That was the last thing I ever said to Ashley.

We live seven miles from the city. On Ashley's trip in to her game, she had a one car wreck. Her car rolled one time, and she was killed. She wasn't speeding, texting, drinking, or talking on the phone. The weather was perfect, the roads were perfect, and there was no traffic. The sun was not in an area where it would affect your vision. In other words, everything was the way it was supposed to be. Nothing should have happened, but it did. To this day, we don't know exactly what happened. I say that because the lower control arm of Ashley's car came loose. Six years after her accident, the car manufacturer issued a recall for that part, indicating that the defect could cause a loss in steering. We don't know if that is what happened, or if a rabbit ran in front of the car, or if Ashley just reached down for something and veered off the road and then overcorrected the car. All we do know, is that Ashley was gone.

As I mentioned earlier, I was coming in also to go to Ashley's game. I drove up on the accident. The police were already there. They had been called by a farmer who witnessed the wreck. Ashley was laying in the field. I still wake up sometimes at night from reliving those next moments. I can still feel my heart beating through my chest, and feel myself running toward her. I know there were emergency personnel around, but I don't remember seeing any of them. I just saw Ashley.

The state trooper told me that he thought Ashley's neck was broken. I called my wife. I remember her answering the phone while she was joking around with someone in her office. I remember telling her to be quiet. I told her that Ashley had been in a wreck and where we were. I know my wife arrived at the scene, but I don't know how.

Meantime, the EMS crew loaded Ashley into the ambulance. She didn't have a pulse. Right before they started to take her to the hospital to pronounce her dead, they located a faint pulse. We still thought we were just following them to the local hospital, but they didn't take the normal turn. I called the sheriff. Since I was the elected D.A., the sheriff and I were good friends. He told me they were taking Ashley to the medical trauma hospital some 40 miles away. We followed behind. At one moment, they stopped and the police were stopping traffic from all directions on the four lane divided highway. They had called for the emergency helicopter to transport Ashley. The helicopter met us on the highway. Jerry and I watched them transfer Ashley to the helicopter, and then we drove the rest of the way there.

I just remember bits and pieces of everything after that. I do remember that the hospital was full of people there for us. I mean so much so that the hospital guest services director talked to me about relocating some of the people. There were people in several waiting rooms. I wish today that I would have gotten a video or written list of people there, so I could properly thank everyone who came to the hospital.

After several hours, the doctor told us that Ashley was not going to make it, and that we could say our final goodbyes. I hated that moment. I know it was the nice thing to do, but I just couldn't take it. They had cleaned up her injuries, but I could still see some blood around her ear. She was not conscious, and I just didn't feel like I was talking to Ashley. After that private time, it was all over. Ashley was again gone, almost like earlier in the day when I was with her in the cotton field.

I know we went home. I really don't remember how or when. I know that I went with my brother the next day to buy a cemetery plot. I do remember that. And, I remember going to the funeral home and trying to make decisions as to caskets, pallbearers, and the service, etc. No mom or dad should ever have to do that for any of their children.

I remember all my family was at our house. Each year

we meet with my family to celebrate Christmas. This year we were to meet at my mom's house in Abilene, Texas. In fact, we were leaving for Abilene on the 29th of December, when Ashley's tournament was over. Instead, everyone was at my house for a funeral. I remember all those Christmas gifts were still unopened at the house.

Countless friends of Ashley came by our home. Also, several attorneys that I knew visited. Others brought food, and just stopped by to show us they cared. All of the events are just a blur to me as I try to remember things.

As I stated earlier, on the 27th, I had returned the last gift Ashley ever got me, that bright tie. I had one of Ashley's friends buy that tie back for me. I wore it to Ashley's funeral. I did get up and speak at the funeral, and to this day I really don't know how I did that. It was probably the largest funeral ever in our community. They opened up every area of the biggest church in town to accommodate people. The police escort to the grave site was over a mile long with police cars. I remember thinking how nice it was for the officers I worked with on a daily basis to do something like that.

After that, it was back to reality, but a different reality now. Nothing was the same. I can tell you that until something like this happens, you never realize just how often it occurs in the world around us.

Without exaggerating, at least once a week, if not more, there is a news story about a teenager involved in a rollover accident. Those stories always make my wife and I pause and remember, even to this day.

It seems as if in nearly every other movie we watch, there is a teenager hurt or killed. Artists write songs about kids dying young. Kenny Chesney wrote "Who You'd Be Today." The Band Perry wrote "If I Die Young." Mindy Smith wrote "One Moment More." Just song after song, it never ends.

When I go away on a vacation or legal seminar, I am constantly asked how many kids I have. That is such a hard question to answer. If I say "2," I have to explain and then the person that asked feels bad. If I say "1," then I feel like I am trying to leave Ashley out, which I don't want to do either.

Every holiday after Ashley's death brings back memories. Father's Day, Mother's Day, Christmas, and Ashley's birthday are probably the toughest.

I also need to mention all of Ashley's friends. I don't want to lose touch with them. They meant the world to Ashley. It is tough though to see them graduate, or get married, or have children, and know that Ashley should have gotten to do those things too. I remember at the high school graduation of Ashley's class, they asked us if they could leave an empty chair for Ashley. It was a nice gesture, but it was difficult to see that chair.

I will never get to walk Ashley down the aisle or hold her child. I won't be able to watch her grow into the young woman who would have made any father proud.

One of the hardest things to endure was not being able to comfort my wife. Jerry would wake up in the middle of the night and go into a different room to cry. I know she was trying to not wake me or bother me, but I could always hear her. I couldn't get up and do anything or say anything. The main reason for my inaction was because at other times, I was doing the same thing. It was so difficult. I didn't know what to do or say to make things better.

Like a fumble in a football game, it just all piled on me. I just could not handle it. All of the above made me go deeper and deeper into my BURNOUT.

Chapter 3

Did they just say 24 million?

In 1996, we successfully prosecuted two defendants for killing a convenience store clerk named Angie Cruz. Angie was shot nine times, all for a grand total of about $300.00 in cash and coin. In other words, it was a perfect example of another senseless crime. Angie left behind a husband, four children, sisters and brothers, and parents.

Two separate juries reached the same result on each defendant – guilty. Both defendants were assessed life in prison. Both defendants appealed their sentences, and both were unsuccessful in their appeals.

Then, several years later, in what is called a habeas petition, both defendants again sought to be released. This time, they had help. Three of the four original attorneys who represented the defendants in their trials filed affidavits with the court indicating that they had provided ineffective counsel; in other words, that they did a bad job.

For those of you not familiar with the legal system, filing an affidavit stating that you were ineffective has become a common occurrence in the past few years. Early in my legal career, attorneys would defend their reputation and their representation. Now, some of them choose to "fall on their sword." Enough attorneys have done so, that a term has been coined for their affidavits; they are called "roll-over" affidavits. One of the three attorneys in our case would later testify that the affidavit is "just another tactic" to try and get the defendant released from custody. The insinuation obviously was that the attorney didn't think that he actually did a bad job, he just said he did to get his client out of prison.

Long story short, the attorney's "tactic" paid off. The highest criminal court in Texas reversed the earlier guilty verdicts citing that the defendants' attorneys did not provide effective assistance of counsel.

So, the newly released defendants sued their counsel, right? I mean after all, those attorneys admitted they had failed the defendants. The highest court in Texas agreed that the attorneys were ineffective. So, those attorneys got sued. Of course not, the defendants sued the Texas Rangers, the local law enforcement, and they sued me.

The defendants were represented by a law firm out of Dallas in their lawsuit. That law firm began to try to influence the public through the media. Although no court had ever made a determination that their clients didn't commit the crime, the attorneys told anybody that would listen that their clients were innocent. Heck, they even created a website touting their innocence.

Earlier, I mentioned that this lawsuit occurred several

years later after the murder in 1996. Well, most of the proceedings also occurred after my daughter Ashley was killed too. At the same time that I was dealing with my daughter's death, I was defending this habeas petition/federal lawsuit. In fact, the lead opposing counsel cross examined me on one occasion regarding how it was possible that I did not remember a certain event. The event to which he referred was a motion that I signed within a few months after Ashley was killed. I didn't remember anything from that time period, and the attorney huffed and puffed how he did not see how that was possible – really?

The proceedings continued for the next six years. I attended deposition after deposition, answered questions, spent time away from my office meeting with attorneys, and all the while still dealt with the daily workload in the office.

When I was deposed for seven hours, I had to discuss my BURNOUT issues. I was asked if I had thought about retiring and, if so, why. I had to explain in front of everyone present, and on video, how Ashley's death had made me burn out on life.

Finally, the proceedings culminated with a federal jury trial in the summer of 2011. The trial lasted six weeks. On the first day of trial, the attorneys told the prospective jurors that they were suing all of us in law enforcement for 24 million dollars. Seriously, did they just say 24 million? I can remember that I wanted to sink down in my seat when I heard that. I calculated it out in my head, that it would take nearly 200 years at my salary to pay that amount of money. The amount seemed as ridiculous as the lawsuit.

The attorneys also told the jury that they would show the jury how I could not be telling the truth. They questioned my honesty throughout the trial. I had always had an "open-file" policy in my office. The other side could see my file. All of the witnesses that testified affirmed that they knew I had this policy. At one point in the trial however, one of the opposing attorneys actually had the gall to state that my "open-file" policy was still subject to what I put in the file. In other words, he was again questioning my integrity.

During my two days of testimony, the attorney questioned me about not attending one of the depositions. I think he asked the question on purpose, just to see how I would react. Earlier I mentioned that I attended several depositions prior to trial. It just so happened that the attorneys scheduled one of the depositions on December 28th, the anniversary date of Ashley's death. I complained to my attorneys, but the other side did not reschedule. Since Ashley's death, I have not worked on December 28th. I seriously doubt I will ever work on that date again in my lifetime. So, I did not attend that particular deposition. At trial, after the attorney had given me a hard time about not attending that deposition, my attorney asked me why I did not go. I broke down on the witness stand and had to tell the entire courtroom about what had happened to Ashley. In that courtroom was all the media, a federal judge, the attorneys, the jury, and a large group of onlookers, including my wife. They all got to see me cry.

The six week trial finally ended with a 119-page charge

from the judge, and a 3-4 hour verdict from the jury. The jury found that none of us in law enforcement were liable for anything. Thankfully for me, I was represented by some unbelievable people and the jury verdict was zero, not 24 million. In fact, the judge later ordered the defendants to pay our costs.

Over the years, I have had a great relationship with several criminal defense attorneys. They have been in my home, come to hear me preach, prayed with me, and we have eaten and visited together. I wondered if those defense attorneys would believe the media hype or believe my past actions. Thankfully, they are true friends and we remain close. However, those outside that circle don't know anything except what they have heard and read in the news.

The verdict was a great relief, but the damage had been done. I had worked my entire legal career trying to do the right thing, and now my reputation was tarnished.

The entire ordeal further exacerbated my BURNOUT. I was to the point where I didn't want to go to work or be out in public at all.

Chapter 4

Epiphany

I had now lived through what most experts claim is the worst loss imaginable – the death of a child. Coupled with that, I had been sued for 24 million dollars just for doing my job. Needless to say, I was definitely experiencing BURNOUT. I probably had every symptom that any psychologist had ever thought of or written down..........and then some.

When I was first elected as the County & District Attorney, my first hire was Laney Dickey. In Laney's employment application, she listed her reason for leaving her previous employment as "there was not enough work to do." That statement made me feel comfortable hiring Laney as my victim coordinator/secretary/receptionist/hot check collector/notary public. I was not disappointed. Laney has been in my office ever since.

We keep a journal in my office, which I will discuss in more detail later in the book. After Ashley's death, Laney had written in the journal that I was mad at her three-fourths of every day, and she was tired of it. This is the same Laney mentioned earlier that did several jobs in my office. It is the same Laney that covered for me when I was out of the office, helped clean our house for us when Ashley was killed, and that helped to edit this book. The strange thing was, that I could see myself being mad or rude, but I could not help myself. I was not a happy camper. Everything and everyone made me mad.

My wife Jerry and I dealt with everything differently. She used work and I abused work. She was already working full-time when Ashley was killed, and then took classes and became a realtor too. She worked all the time. I couldn't make myself go to work. I would go to work late and leave early. I got elected to be the D.A. If I had been an employee, and not elected, I would have been fired. I would work on nights and weekends when there was nobody around, and that was comfortable to me. I enjoyed that. My office staff laughed that I was the Night Crew.

I have always been a "people person." I love meeting and visiting with new people. But now, I didn't want to see, meet, or visit with anyone.

I always took pride in my leadership. I was the kind of boss that treated employees right. My mom and dad had taught me that virtue early on in life. I don't care who you are, or how much or little money you have, you treat everyone the same. If I took a half day or day off, then I made sure my employees got to do the same. I let my employees go to any of their children's school functions, I gave them shopping days for Christmas, and I always gave them credit for anything good that happened in our office.

After Ashley's death, all that changed. I now didn't care if I "evened it up" on days off. If I let them attend school functions or be out of the office for any reason, I would also leave. I just closed the office. I didn't care what the public thought. Now, as a credit to my employees, they still cared and kept the office open.

When I was at work, I wasn't really there. I just didn't care what happened. Our office's reputation around the state is that we are one of the best prosecution offices for protecting victim's rights. We listen to our victims, we keep them informed, we go the extra mile for them. Basically, we put them first. Now, I had to depend upon my staff for that job. I wanted to care about their needs, but now it didn't come as naturally to me as it had in the past. Now, I had to work at it.

I read all kinds of books about BURNOUT and depression. I even went and took a battery of tests to determine if I needed help. The answer was of course "yes," but I didn't pursue it further. I have never been a big believer in counseling or medication. After all, I am a guy, and I am from West Texas. I just don't believe that I can take a pill and everything will be alright. So, I didn't.

I put on a good front. Everyone would comment on how well I was doing, and how they couldn't believe how well I was coping. Everyone, that is, except those closest to me. They knew, and so did I. Thankfully, for them -- my closest family and friends – I finally started to come out of it.

By that time though, it was time for a change for me. I decided not to seek re-election, and try something else. But what? I had no idea. Early on, I even considered staying at home and doing nothing. We were at a point money-wise that I could do that, and Jerry worked all the time anyway. I wouldn't have to be around people, and that seemed pretty appealing to me. Slowly, I recognized how selfish that would be. Not only was it selfish to my wife, but I didn't believe God put me on this earth to barricade myself in my house and watch *Netflix* movies all day long. There had to be something else for me.

People asked me almost daily what I was going to do next. I jokingly told some that I would be an activities director for a *Sandals* resort. My wife and I had been several times, and I actually thought I would be good at that. I gave serious consideration to being a travel agent. A friend of mine, Amy McHugh, is one of the best *Sandals* agents around, and we had discussed that I could come to work with her at her company, Dream Makers Vacation Services. I love planning trips, and have done so for several friends and family members. Maybe this was the path I needed to take. After all, it would be helping people.

I was so confused, and finally did what I should have done at first. I started praying. I can't tell you how much I prayed about my decision, but it was a lot. I also fasted. Do we move to Florida or Jamaica, do I stay at home, or become a travel agent?

You know, God doesn't always answer prayers like you think He will, but I do think He helped me with my next step. I decided to try and list my spiritual gifts. In the Bible, Romans 12: 6-8 teaches that we all possess gifts from God. And, we don't all have the same gifts. I figured if I could get a good assessment of my gift(s), it would help me decide my future. I asked Laney what her opinion was as well. Laney's list was longer than mine, but I expected that, (1) because she is a nice person, and (2) because I pay her! A few traits that we both listed were: public speaking, list making, sense of humor, honesty, and not afraid to share life. I still didn't know what to do with that. Then, my Epiphany!

I know, I said no big words, and then I go and title this chapter "Epiphany." On the early morning of December 8, 2011, I had an epiphany. It was just like a light bulb going off in my head. I got up, started writing, and it was as if God was telling me what to do. It was the most direct answer to prayer I had ever received. I just knew I was going to speak about my life and my struggles with BURNOUT. That is also when the F.I.N.G.E.R. philosophy came to me. I literally wrote down everything by 8 o'clock that morning. I started writing this book within a day, and finished the first draft within ten days.

I just knew I was going to write this book and become a motivational speaker. But what did I know about doing either of those things? I have barely ever written anything in my lifetime, including my high school term papers. I am sure my mom can vouch for that. I do speak all the time in public to judges for hearings, to juries during trials, and for Walk Thru the Bible seminars that I have conducted — but never anything like this.

When I first told my wife, her initial response was hilarious. She said, "Do you see the irony?" Of course, she was referring to that fact that I was going to be a motivational speaker, when I was burned out and not motivated to do anything.

Then I thought about my favorite person in the Bible. I love Mordecai. When Haman is plotting to kill all the Jews, Mordecai asked Esther to intervene, but Esther was scared. If she petitioned the king, it could mean her death. In Esther 4:14, Mordecai asks Esther "How do you know God didn't put you in this position, for such a time as this?"

I have asked high school kids in the past, how do they know God didn't put their locker next to someone for such a time as this? Even when we are at the grocery store, how do we know that God didn't put us there at just that time in order to help someone else? So, how did I know God didn't do the same for me? I had been praying for an answer, fasting for an answer, and he gave me an answer. I don't know if this was the answer I had sought, but it was the answer that I received.

After all, if your sink is leaking, you call a plumber because you want somebody that has experience with the problem. Well, if you need help with BURNOUT issues, what better expert than somebody who can relate to what you are experiencing? You need advice from someone who has been through the same things you are experiencing.

It was time I shared my story. It was time I shared my F.I.N.G.E.R. philosophy that helped me.

Hence the next chapters.................

Chapter 5

F

F is for fun.

In November, 1997, I hired Scott Say to work as my Assistant County & District Attorney. Scott was a hardworking local attorney. He put himself through law school by working various jobs. He had a family, and was looking for a change. He was a great fit for my office.

In March of 2001, Scott had worked in my office for a little over three years. In his office on his bookshelf, he had a beautiful glass bottle that was half full of 18 year old scotch. Or, at least until that spring day, it contained scotch. Laney and I decided to play a prank on Scott. While he was out, we replaced the scotch with cream soda. In case you ever want to try this at home, the colors are almost exactly the same. Then we waited, and waited, and waited. We just knew that he would celebrate a trial victory or something with a drink from the bottle. He never did. After nearly two years, we finally had to tell him what we had done!

Later that same year, what came to be known as the great doughnut caper happened in our office. When grand jury meets in our county, our District Clerk provides the grand jurors with doughnuts. After one meeting, there was a doughnut left over. I brought it to Laney. She didn't want it. It ended up in my desk drawer. Then it appeared in Scott's file cabinet. It went from there to Laney's purse, to my lunch box, and all over the office for the next two weeks. Finally, the molded doughnut was gone – or, at least I thought it was gone. It was no longer in our office.

I was headed to some court proceeding one day, and stopped at the mailbox and got the mail before going into the courtroom. The mailbox was centrally located on the first floor of our courthouse. There it was, the doughnut had been mailed to me. I took it from the mailbox, and carried it down the hall, all the while talking to several attorneys. Needless to say, it was just a little bit embarrassing. After that, the doughnut's final resting place was in a little opening in the middle of the steering wheel of Laney's vehicle.

The point is, that I have always tried to have **FUN** in whatever I do. I am a big believer in laughter. After all, laughter is the best medicine. Although, as Randy on *My Name is Earl* put it: "Whoever said laughter is the best medicine, never had gonorrhea!"

There are studies after studies that show how laughter helps not only mentally, but also physically. The best benefit of laughter is that it reduces stress. It takes your mind away from stressful situations. It is difficult to be burned out when you make laughter a regular part of every day.

Some of my favorite quotes on having fun and laughter are:

Laughter is an instant vacation. ~Milton Berle

Laughter is the shortest distance between two people. ~Victor Borge

What soap is to the body, laughter is to the soul. ~Yiddish Proverb

When people are laughing, they're generally not killing each other. ~Alan Alda

A man isn't poor if he can still laugh. ~Raymond Hitchcock

A good time to laugh is any time you can. ~Linda Ellerbee

Seven days without laughter makes one weak. ~Mort Walker

A laugh is a smile that bursts. ~Mary H. Waldrip

Laughter is the sun that drives winter from the human face. ~Victor Hugo

Carry laughter with you wherever you go. ~Hugh Sidey

Laughter is a tranquilizer with no side effects. ~Arnold Glasow

I also believe humor is biblical. When Sarah finds out she is going to have a baby, she laughs. I don't know if my wife would laugh or cry if she found out she was pregnant at 90 years of age. Ecclesiastes 3:4, along with the Byrds, both point out that there is a time to laugh. Proverbs 17:22 says, "A joyful heart is good medicine, but a crushed spirit dries up the bones."

Also, there are so many funny stories in the Bible. In II Kings 2:24, God hears Elijah, and sends two bears to attack the kids making fun of Elijah's bald head. It's hard not to laugh at that unless, of course, you were one of those unlucky 42 offenders.

When David presents 200 Philistine foreskins to Saul for his daughter's hand in marriage, you don't know whether to laugh or double over. I mean how did David present the foreskins, gift wrapped? It reminds you of the little kid on *America's Funniest Videos* hitting his dad in the groin with a baseball bat. You know it hurts, but you have to laugh.

In I Kings, Elijah asks the false Baal prophets if Baal is out sleeping, or too busy, or on a journey, when they cannot bring down fire. Several biblical scholars believe "on a journey" in this context refers to going to the bathroom. Basically, Elijah asks the prophets if Baal is too busy in the bathroom to bring down fire. As Larry the Cable Guy would say, " That is funny, I don't care who you are."

Biblical stories such as the big, fat Eglon getting stabbed in the bathroom, and Moses making the golden calf offenders drink their disgrace, are just a few of the other numerous examples of humor in the Bible.

I know that it is hard to believe, but you can also find fun and laughter at work, even when you prosecute sex offenders and murderers for a living. In fact, it is stressful situations like that when you need to find time to laugh the most.

Some of the funniest times in my work were:

–   I had a kid come in to pay on his hot checks in my office. He owed a lot of money. As he paid cash in hundred dollar bills to my secretary, I went over to give him a hard time. I playfully asked, "What did you do, rob a bank?" He had the strangest look on his face when I said that. Sure enough, a few days later, we found out that he had robbed a local grocery store safe. At least he was conscientious enough to come pay us what he owed!

– I once prosecuted a sex offender with the last name of FEELER.

– I have prosecuted two grandmothers for delivery of cocaine. One was in her 70s and one in her 80s. One would take the cocaine out of her panties and ask, "What can granny get you?" The other asked officers what the problem was, "I only sell to adults, not children."

– I had an assault case on one sister fighting with her other sister, and biting her sister's nipple.

– I had a large woman drop her drawers in front of Laney to show Laney where she was burned with a curling iron during an assault. Laney said that is something that once you have seen it, you can never un-see it.

– I had one girl tamper with her urine test results. Sounds normal, right? Well, this girl knew her test results would be okay, so she tampered with them to get *in* trouble. She wanted to go back to jail, because her boyfriend was there in jail. You just can't make this stuff up.

– We had a child sexual assault victim tell us one time that the defendant had a mole on his penis. We obtained a search warrant to make him have to strip down in front of several officers and let them take photos. Sure enough, there was a mole, and he got a trip to the penitentiary. I don't know which was worse for him, having several officers laugh at his penis, or being confined in the penitentiary.

– A defendant robbed a lady in our jurisdiction and tied her up with his belt. Only problem for him, it was a western belt with his name on it. As Bill Engvall would say, "Here's your sign."

– We were prosecuting a girl one time for forgery. She just happened to be a stripper. She found out in court one day that she would be going to jail. We went to my office to call her attorney, and I turned one way and she ran the other. She left the courthouse and proceeded to flag down cars by lifting up her shirt. She was successful getting some unsuspecting guy to give her a ride (no pun intended), and was not arrested until several weeks later.

– A defendant was arrested for crack cocaine possession. When taken to jail and searched, it was discovered that he had crack cocaine in the crack of his buttocks. The famous Crack-in-the-Crack case. It was always fun to ask the officers how they cracked that case. I did think it would be an effective "Just Say No" to drugs campaign, to take a photo of where the drugs were before users bought them.

–   There was a guy in my jurisdiction that routinely beat up his wife. He came home drunk one night and broke his wife's nose. She finally had enough. She took a knife out of the kitchen drawer and began to stab him. The neighbors heard the yelling and called the police. When the police arrived, the wife had the husband down on the ground in the front yard, and was choking him with a water hose. You know, I don't remember ever filing a case against her!

–   Law enforcement stopped a man one night, and he knew he had an outstanding misdemeanor warrant for his arrest. Therefore, when the officer approached him, he gave the officer his brother's name as his identity. Only problem – his brother had an outstanding warrant for a *felony* offense.

–   A juvenile was sentenced to a detention facility. As he was exiting the courtroom, the juvenile took off running. He ran down the hall, down the stairs, and through another courthouse office. The only problem for him was that the opposite door of the office he ran to had already been locked. He bounced off that locked door like a basketball off a gym floor. The judge and I had been chasing the juvenile. But for the locked door, we never would have caught him. It still took us time to reach him as we tried to catch our breath from running. Needless to say, neither of us were in the best shape.

I have dozens of funny stories like the ones listed above that we have written down in our office journal. We see a lot of things that "normal" people don't know goes on around them, and that people don't need to know happens. Whenever we get one of those really bad cases, it is always good to go back and look at some of the funny examples from the past.

You also have to be able to laugh at yourself. I was just out of undergraduate school and working at a bank in the Dallas/Fort Worth metroplex. I was turning 25 years old, and life was good. All of my co-workers threw a birthday party for me at work; things could not be better. Hold on, yes they could. Because, on the way home my day just continued to improve. As I drove in rush hour traffic, something strange started to happen. A car pulled up beside me and a young, beautiful girl honked her horn at me and waved. I waved back and didn't really think much about it. Until, that is, another girl honked at me. This happened a few more times before I got home that evening. I had a gleam in my eye as I told my wife what had happened. I told her that I didn't know if it was because I was older or just looking good that day, but girls were noticing me and it felt pretty good. We ate dinner, and as I usually did, I went outside to play basketball on the hoop above our garage door. As I passed my car parked in the garage, I noticed something. Yes, you guessed it. My co-workers had placed two big signs on the back of my car that read, "Honk Twice, Today is my Birthday." Since I approached my car from the front when I left work, I had not seen the signs until that moment. We laughed then, and everyone that participated in the prank still laughs about it today.

You have to be able to have fun. For those of us with BURNOUT, this is much easier said than done. I just mentioned a few paragraphs earlier how we kept a journal in our office. Well, in that journal, Laney had made an entry that stated the following:

"10-18-05 ..... Today is the first day that Mark smiled or laughed, it was like the old Mark was back."

Ashley's death was in December, 2004, and the first time I smiled or laughed at work after that was October of 2005, nearly a year later.

When you suffer BURNOUT, nothing seems funny. Sometimes you may have to force yourself to have fun. Funny *Youtube* videos are a good way to force yourself to laugh. It is also important to make co-workers take the time to have fun and laugh with you. They may not want to do this, because when you are at work they are hoping to actually get some work done. Also, your co-workers may have given up on trying to laugh with you if they have tried to for awhile, and you haven't been receptive. Remember, it took me ten months to laugh again at work.

Lastly, having fun is contagious. If you see something funny, you want to share it with others. If you are sharing it with others, then you are necessarily "with others." Anytime you can avoid the isolation of BURNOUT, it helps your recovery.

BURNOUT zaps the life out of you. Humor and laughter can help bring you back to life. It is difficult to feel sorry for yourself when you are laughing and having fun. Fun and laughter are the best therapy for your BURNOUT.

Chapter 6

I

I is for important.

My wife and I, like most parents, are extremely proud of our son. Alex has a gift for just about everything. One thing in particular is public speaking. Even when he was young he had that gift. As is often the case, our church leaders would allow the young boys of the church to recite a Bible verse. Whenever it was Alex's turn, he would receive the verse at the beginning of our meeting, memorize it, and then get up without his Bible and recite the verse. He would also tell everyone in the congregation, "Hello." It used to scare me to death, worrying that he would forget the scripture. It just came naturally for him.

He has been fortunate to give a high school graduation speech and a law school graduation speech. I still have people come up and tell me that both were the best speeches they have ever heard, and the high school speech was over 8 years ago. Even more impressive, the people telling me this are not relatives!

Alex ended both graduation speeches with the same story. He told the graduates to imagine their lives as juggling four balls. Those balls are: (1) your faith, (2) your family, (3) your friends, and (4) your work. The fourth ball is made out of rubber. If you drop it, it bounces right back to you. However, the first three balls are made out of glass. Don't ever drop those balls. The point obviously to the juggling story is to hold on tight to your faith, family, and friends. Those are the most important things in your life. You can always find a new job. Your work is not as important as the other three things.

Alex is so right. You have to remember what is

IMPORTANT. Without faith, I just don't know how anyone can face BURNOUT issues, or any issues for that matter. We all need the reminder of putting God first. He is the most important thing in our lives.

My dad had a plaque hanging in his office. It read: "If you were accused of being a Christian, would there be enough evidence to prove it?" As a Christian, and as a prosecutor, I have always loved that plaque. Since my dad's death, the plaque now hangs in my office as a constant reminder for me.

People need to see your faith. Remember the children's song and don't "hide it under a bushel." It is difficult sometimes as a BURNOUT victim to show your faith to people. First, people need to see you. As we have already discussed, when suffering from BURNOUT you are around people less and less. Then, when people do see you, it is often difficult to share anything with them, much less your faith.

One of the most difficult things for me during my BURNOUT was attending church. I have to admit that I struggled with my faith after Ashley was killed. I just kept asking "WHY?" As a result of that struggle, I began to attend church less and less.

As I previously mentioned, the song Ashley played on the piano the night before she was killed was "Listen to our Hearts." I loved that song. Now, every time we sang it in church, either my wife or I had to get up and leave because it made us so emotional.

It was also difficult for me to visit with others. For some reason that I still don't understand, that was especially true for church. I quit attending as many meetings, I quit attending our "potluck" meals, and I quit having people over in my home. In short, I quit being a good spiritual leader in my home.

The best way to be re-energized is to be in the Word. And, the best way to be in the Word is to gather with other friends and family who believe as you do. It is possible to read the Bible at home. In fact, we all should be doing that. However, in reality that rarely happens. You can set aside time to watch a sermon or lesson online, but invariably something distracts you from that.

It is beneficial for the health of all of us to actually get out and be with other Christians, but it is especially good for BURNOUT victims. In fact, I believe that small group settings are the best medicine for those of us suffering. Those settings are not as rigid as a more formal meeting, and allow us to open up more.

One of the most difficult things to do for BURNOUT victims is to talk to others about their situation. It is embarrassing. However, if you can develop a close group of like-minded Christians around you, it makes you more comfortable to share your struggles. I believe strongly in the power of prayer. If you are suffering from BURNOUT, it is extremely important to harness that power through your small group's prayers on your behalf.

The second of the important juggling balls is your family. If you are blessed with a wonderful, caring family, take advantage of that. And no, I don't mean hit them up for a loan. I mean share your struggles, just as you would with your church small group.

Your family have had to put up with your BURNOUT symptoms the most. You have been rude to them, ignored them, and shut them out. They see and tolerate your symptoms daily.

Your family knows you inside and out. They have been there for the good times, as well as the bad. If your BURNOUT was a result of a loss of a loved one, then they are experiencing the same feelings that you are experiencing.

I think my lawsuit was more stressful to my wife and my mother than myself. When you hurt, your family hurts. Just as it is written in I Corinthians 12:26, "If one part of our body hurts, we hurt all over." The same is true for your family.

The last of the important juggling balls is your friends. It is often said that friends are the glue that keep our lives together. That statement is so true for me.

My friends carried me through my BURNOUT. My co-worker friends covered for me at work. Laney and Scott took on extra work and stayed longer hours to make up for me not being there. They cleaned my house when Ashley was killed. They put up with me being angry and rude all the time. They should get a medal for their service.

Attorneys that I knew covered for me as well. Prosecutors from every jurisdiction around mine called to see what they could do to help. Defense attorneys also volunteered their services and, as previously mentioned, did not abandon me when the lawsuit sought to discredit me.

You need all three balls – Faith, Family, and Friends – to recover from BURNOUT. That support system helps when you can't do it on your own.

Chapter 7

N

N is for notes.

One year before Ashley was killed, when she was 15 years old, she was a social butterfly. She was always wanting to go out with her friends. If she wasn't with Mekayla, she was with Jenna. And if she wasn't with one of them, then she was with one of a dozen other running buddies. Ashley wanting to go out all the time was actually a blessing in disguise for us. We definitely used it to our advantage. I can't tell you the number of times we uttered the following phrase to Ashley, "Okay, if you want to go out, you have to clean your room." It was our only remaining leverage. And, it worked like a charm. Or, at least we thought it did.

Ashley would clean her room spotless. However, she defined "room" much like Bill Clinton might define "is" — "room" didn't include her closet. She was piling everything in her closet. While her room looked clean, her closet was a disaster. There was food in there, mixed in with dirty clothes, and most likely homework. I discovered her secret quite by accident one day. As I was walking down the hallway that leads to her bedroom, I smelled smoke. As I tried to trace its origin, it led me closer and closer to Ashley's closet. As I opened the closet doors, the sight was indescribable. The closest I can come to a description for you is for you to close your eyes and imagine what Santa's sleigh looks like prior to giving out any of the toys. There was junk literally from floor to ceiling. Weeks worth of trips out with friends had gathered in one small area. The smell — well, it was smoke. One of Ashley's blouses had melted against the closet ceiling light bulb. We are lucky the entire house didn't burn down.

Ashley may have had me wrapped around her little

finger, but she knew she was in trouble on this one. To this day, I don't remember what punishment I dished out. I can tell you that it wasn't a "time out." What I do remember is what happened next. When I went to bed that night, I had a note on my bed. That note is now framed, and I would like to share it with you:

Dear Father,

Dear Mr. Yarbrough a/k/a father. I apologize for secretly storing my clean/dirty clothes on the bottom raising to the ceiling of the closet. It was very unfunny and somewhat irresponsible of me to withhold you of my secretive sneakiness. From now on, I will either put up my clothes where they belong and keep my closet clean, or I will learn how to make a lock and key so I can continue my cleverness and pile my junk back into my closet so I may continue to be lazy. Either way, I hope this experience taught you a lesson as I know it did me. I beg of you not to hold this occurrence against me and we can "forgive-and-forget" as you know you're only 15 once and your baby girl is growing like a tomato!!

In loving respects
Your daughter a/k/a
Your pride and joy, Ashley

congrats on the trial win!!

As you might imagine, that note means more to me than anything money could buy. And, I have no idea what jury trial I had that week, and couldn't care less.

That is just one example of why I believe it is so important to keep the **NOTES** you receive during your lifetime. As you get older, without the written evidence, you forget those notes and stories that made you laugh or cry or both. If you are suffering from BURNOUT, it is so important to have those notes to help you cope. If your BURNOUT was brought on because of a death of a loved one, then you just want to see anything from them.

We were so lucky in that regard. In addition to the note already mentioned above, on Ashley's 16th birthday, just six months before she was killed, Ashley wrote us her top 16 memories. Some were memories that I hope I will never forget, and some were ones that I didn't even know meant that much to her. Without the note, I would not remember half of the list. She also wrote us homemade birthday cards that we kept. Just one month before she was killed, she wrote me a homemade birthday poem.   I had gotten to where I grounded her for hours instead of days, and boy did it irritate her. I would give her two hours for talking back, four hours for missing curfew, etc. So when my birthday rolled around, this is the poem I received:

My Daddy's Birthday

If you had a dad as good as mine
One that's funny and mighty fine

You'd try to please him every day
And always mind him in every way

On his birthday, you'd make him happy
I think this poem may sound a little sappy

He is my father, and has great powers
Cause he always gives me an extra 6 hours

No more radio! No more T.V.!
No more phone, or internet for me

So - I'm using this poem as a constant plea
I love you Daddy!!! So please love me

May your birthday be the best you've had
Cause you certainly are the #1 Dad

And I might add this is all you get
Until I can get back on the internet!

Love you,

Ashley

Notes are important also if your BURNOUT was brought on because of work. It may not happen very often, but we all get some kind of accolades at work. Somebody takes the time to tell us they appreciate us. Keep those notes. If somebody praises you orally rather than in writing, write down what they said and keep it. You need to be able to have visual proof that you are important; that you made a difference to somebody.

I have kept over 50 notes from work – most from Laney, some from Scott, and some from victims of crime. Once when a jury assessed a defendant a life sentence, I received a plaque from the victim's family whose family member was murdered. They bronzed the actual judgment in the case, and put a note with it: "with deepest thanks for justice served." That plaque and note mean so much to me. Over the years, I have kept both serious and funny notes.

I received what prosecutors call the "ultimate note" from a jury. Other than capital murder cases, the most serious crimes in Texas carry a range of punishment from five years to 99 years or life in the penitentiary. Those serious crimes include normal murder cases, aggravated sexual assault cases, and kidnapping cases, just to name a few. I had prosecuted a murder case before a jury, and was awaiting their verdict. The judge summoned us to the courtroom with a question from the jury. What was their concern? Did they want to hear testimony read back to them? We didn't know. Then the judge read the foreman's note:

"We would like to know the difference between life and 99 years."

As a prosecutor, it just doesn't get any better. At that point, you know the jury isn't thinking about giving the defendant a slap on the wrist. I definitely have held on to that note too. And by the way, there is no difference, and that particular jury chose Life.

I also highly recommend keeping a journal or diary at work. Remember those funny work stories I shared in the chapter on "F" is for fun. I would not have remembered half of those stories had we not kept a journal in our office for several years. Sometimes you need those stories to share with other attorneys when you attend continuing legal education. Other times you need those stories just to review them and remember good times.

When you suffer from BURNOUT, you tend to forget all the good times and just think about the hassles and the problems of work. Those notes can bring you back around.

If your BURNOUT was brought on by family problems, notes can also help there. One of the best ideas I ever heard was from Laney. She recommended keeping a shoe box with a slot cut in the lid. Anytime your child does something funny, or memorable, just write it down and place it in that box. It doesn't need to be anything fancy; it just needs to be handy. We all have good intentions of keeping notes like that in a fancy "baby book." And, when we have our first child, we annotate everything from first words, to first steps, to losing the first tooth. As the years go by, we get caught up with life and forget to pull the book out and make an entry. That holds especially true for second and subsequent children. Those kids are lucky if we write down their height and weight at their birth. The shoe box is much less rigid and easier to do. And, who wants to put a funny memory about a teenager in a baby book?

Trust me, when your kids are teenagers, you need to see visual evidence that they once were actually good kids. It might just keep you from killing them!

One of the most important things you can do for someone suffering from BURNOUT is give them encouragement. The Bible teaches us the importance God places on encouragement. When we meet together at church, we go to worship the Lord. However, we can and should worship the Lord all the time. First Corinthians and Hebrews both teach us the purpose of meeting together is to encourage and edify each other. Sometimes, we all need that extra slap on the back to keep us going. That is especially true for BURNOUT victims. Notes are just one additional way to encourage those suffering from BURNOUT.

Whatever the reason for your BURNOUT, being able to go back and look at notes from the past can help you start looking forward to the future.

Chapter 8

G

G is for giving back.

When I was being sued for 24 million dollars, and going through depositions and being called a liar, life was not fun. However, one day I walked in the office, and it was not Christmas, not my birthday, but just a random day on the calendar. Scott and Laney had gotten me a gift. It was a dart board with one of the lawsuit attorney's photos imprinted onto the board itself. I won't say which attorney, but it was one of the attorneys who was not man enough to congratulate us when he lost the trial and we won. Attorneys know that much like the end of a football game, you always congratulate the other side, either verbally or with a handshake.

No matter how burned out I was from the lawsuit, that gift and the subsequent holes all in it helped bring me back to life. It still ranks as one of the best gifts I have ever received. If you are reading this book at Christmastime, the personalized dartboard is always a crowd favorite.

This chapter is about giving. It is always helpful to give to someone suffering from BURNOUT. It doesn't matter whether you give a Sonic 2 for 1 drink, a special note, a meal, or whatever. It is always nice, whether you suffer from BURNOUT or not, to receive a special gift from others. But, this chapter is actually about **GIVING BACK**. I believe it is more important for the BURNOUT victim to give to others, rather than to receive a gift. Several of us as children were taught the biblical lesson from the book of Acts on giving to others. I believe this especially holds true for BURNOUT.

When I went through my BURNOUT, I was always

thinking about myself. I thought about how rough life was for me, how it wasn't fair, and that I didn't do anything to deserve my lot in life. Giving to others, no matter how small, changes the emphasis. You are no longer thinking just about you, you are thinking of others. That attitude adjustment helps with the recovery. You have to get back in the world to give to others. It makes you concentrate on others, not yourself.

There are so many ways to give back. Give unexpected gifts. You can give unexpected gifts to your co-workers. I had personalized bobble heads made for my co-workers, and everyone still talks about them.

Give things that make people laugh. My co-workers gave me a book entitled: *1001 Ways to Reward Employees*. Or, give things to make people cry. When Ashley was killed, someone we knew donated money in Ashley's name to a program that sends Bibles to people in Africa. Another friend gave us a scrapbook of notes written by others about Ashley. It means the world to my wife and me. We can never thank Kelli Bussanmas enough.

Give to your church. I understand that tithing may be an Old Testament concept, but look at how much Jesus gave back to people in the New Testament. Churches are a great place to give, because you know that the money will be used to further God's kingdom.

Give back when you go on vacations too. My wife and I have visited a resort in Jamaica a few times. Each time, we take school supplies to a local school there. Trust me, you will not have time to think about yourself and your BURNOUT issues when you see kids thrilled to be getting crayons, and stickers, and markers. It will be the highlight of your vacation.

Give to help others. Several months after Ashley's closet fiasco, she boxed up several clothes to give away. When we asked her who she wanted to give the clothing to, she responded, "To the Asian kids." Ashley's comment was almost funny because it was so random. We had no idea what she meant by that statement. One month after Ashley's above statement, and the same week Ashley was killed, a massive tsunami struck Indonesia. It came to be known as the 2004 Indian Ocean tsunami, South Asian tsunami, or Indonesian tsunami. That tsunami killed over 230,000 people, and displaced thousands of Asian children. Humanitarian aid efforts began immediately, requesting water, cash, and clothing. All Jerry and I could think about was Ashley's previous comment. We even contacted the First Lady to try and make sure Ashley's clothes that she had boxed up were donated to the tsunami victims. We believed that although Ashley's statement was a month prior to the disaster, she somehow knew.

Give to your favorite charity, and give to organizations to which you belong. As a prosecutor, there are so many worthy non-profit organizations that I have the pleasure of seeing in action. Two of those are the Children's Protective Services and the Children's Advocacy Center. I am also lucky enough to belong to the largest prosecutor organization in the world, the Texas District and County Attorneys Association (TDCAA). Their foundation is a great place to give back.

Again, I emphasize that it is not as much about giving to BURNOUT victims, but BURNOUT victims giving back. Even small things like buying Girl Scout cookies will help you recover. It is hard to isolate yourself from society when you are giving to others. Do it because it is the right thing to do, but also do it because it is the important thing to do for your well-being.

One of the best ways to give back as a BURNOUT victim is to share your story with someone else who is struggling. I have sent out countless letters to people I have never met. The letters are all to parents who have lost a child or children in a car accident. I see their story on the news, and send them a letter within a few days. The letter invariably discusses things that I have learned that I think will benefit them in the next few days, weeks, or months. They are things that you might not think about, unless you too have unfortunately suffered such a loss.

Before you start giving me a medal for being such a nice guy, it wasn't my idea. Actually, I did decide to send the letters out to those parents, but I learned how to share my story from a friend named Steve Stokes.

Steve Stokes and I are old friends. He and I attended law school together. Most students go straight to law school from undergraduate school. Steve and I did not. We had both been out in the real world for awhile before going to law school. That, coupled with the fact that both of our dads had farmed, and that both of us enjoyed watching high school basketball, made us form a friendship that continues to this day.

Ten years and one day before our daughter Ashley was killed, Steve and his wife Vicki lost their son Chris to a hunting accident. Chris was 16 years of age at the time of his death, just like Ashley. Steve and Vicki also had one other child, Jeff. It was almost eerie how similar things were for both families.

I already mentioned that I don't recall much about what happened at the hospital that day of Ashley's death. However, I do remember Steve calling me. I think he and Vicki were in California, but he wanted to share some thoughts and a prayer with me. Later, Steve and Vicki met with Jerry and me. That is a meeting that no two sets of parents should ever have to attend. They shared so many stories with us as to what we could expect. I bet they gave us 10-20 books to read on the subject of the death of a child. Everything they told us, happened to us. They just seemed to know what would happen.

As much as they helped us, it had to bring up some painful memories for them. But, in a true Christian manner, they didn't let that stop them from being there for us. Expressing my heartfelt thanks to them in this book is just one of the many ways that I have attempted to show them how much they helped Jerry and me.

You never know, when you share your BURNOUT pain with someone in a similar situation, how it could change their life. Don't ever pass up an opportunity that God places in front of you to give back, whether in words or deeds.

64

Chapter 9

E

E is for escape.

No book would be complete without consulting America's modern day expert on just about every subject. Yes of course, I am referring to Adam Sandler. Remember in Sandler's movie, *Happy Gilmore*, how Happy was struggling with his putter? Golfers know you drive for show and putt for dough. Remember how Stubbs helped Happy? He told him to go to his happy place. The screen fades and you can see Happy's happy place – a garden with his girlfriend in lingerie and a pitcher of beer in each hand, a small guy riding a tricycle, and Happy's grandmother winning at the slot machines. Stubbs asked Happy how he felt, and Happy said "Better." Not to ruin the ending for those who have mistakenly not seen the movie, but Shooter McGavin didn't stand a chance after that.

Escaping to your happy place does make you feel better. I am sure not all of us would have the same daydream as Happy Gilmore, but you need to be able to **ESCAPE**. It doesn't matter if the escape is real like a vacation, or just a daydream.

When Ashley was killed, Jerry and I escaped on "miniature" vacations once a month for the next year. Mostly, we just took a short two or three day trip somewhere, just to get away. We just needed to be able to escape reality. Life was so hard, we just needed out of the pressure.

After my lawsuit, we escaped to the mountains of Utah, on the advice of and with the assistance of my attorney.

I have escaped by skydiving in Las Vegas, zip-lining in Jamaica, and swimming with sharks in the Bahamas. One of the most unique ways that I have escaped is by swimming with pigs in the Exuma Islands. You won't think too much about your daily stress or BURNOUT when you are in crystal clear waters while feeding bread crumbs to huge swimming pigs.

Vacations are a biblical way to Escape. Recall in the book of Genesis, how Abraham vacationed with Sarah, Lot, and Terah. Abraham journeyed all the way to the promised land. And you thought Chevy Chase went a long way in the movie *Vacation*. Further, Noah is the first person we know about that went on a cruise. Calling Abraham's and Noah's journeys "vacations" is meant as a tongue-in-cheek comment. However, the Bible does provide examples of ways to escape.

One of those biblical ways is to escape with prayer. Jesus escapes from his disciples in the garden of Gethsemane to pray. Prayer is your opportunity to tell God about your struggles. When you suffer from BURNOUT, sometimes you cannot share your problems with anyone but God. In my darkest times, the best and only way I was able to escape was to turn to God in prayer.

You can also escape without ever leaving. I believe that the Spanish have figured it out. Their culture started siestas. This nap after the midday meal is brilliant. Maybe they started it as way of protection from the afternoon sun, but the reason behind it is not important to me. Daily rest helps to invigorate you. It helps you cope with anything that comes your way in the afternoon.

While rest helps to invigorate you, exercising helps to motivate you. Exercising is recommended for your physical well-being, but it is also essential for your mental health. Participating in team sports is a good way to reconnect with others that you may have been avoiding. Also, individual workouts are a helpful way to escape by taking your mind off of your BURNOUT issues. If you are feeling depressed, then a strenuous workout would help. Whereas, if you are under an extreme amount of stress, then a light walk might help.

Another way you can escape without ever leaving is to have a photo in your office of a time or place that automatically takes you back there. A spot where all is good in the world. With just one glance at that photo, you are instantly transported back to that time and place.

For me, that happy place is a photo of my feet, as I lay on a chair on a beach in Jamaica, facing the turquoise waters with only a yellow beach umbrella blocking my view. Every time I look at that photo, I am back on that beach. I have a copy of that photo in my office, at my house, and on my *Facebook* page profile.

Your photo may be of a museum painting, or of a ride at Disney World, or a golf course in Scotland. The content is not important, as long as when you look at the photo, any stress you have just seems to wash away and you are transported to a better place and time.

It is not only a good thing to be able to escape to your happy place, but it is also very important for BURNOUT victims to escape from their home. Most BURNOUT victims want to be by themselves in their home all the time. They want the isolation and the comfort of lounge pants and freedom from the outside world.

While isolating yourself might seem like it keeps you happy, in reality it is bringing you deeper and deeper into BURNOUT. It's like a mousetrap for a mouse. That cheese sure looks inviting. Don't do it – run the other way.

The more you stay home, the more you want to stay home. The more you want to stay home, the less likely you are to communicate with others. The less you communicate with others, the less likely you are to ever be of service to anyone else. God didn't put you on this Earth to be trapped in your own home just thinking about yourself and your problems all day, every day. God wants you to be an example for others, to serve others, and to share his Word. Isolating yourself at home doesn't serve any of those purposes. Escape from that trap.

Also, be careful not to escape by abusing food, drugs, or alcohol. Much like staying at home is a way of escape, abusing food, drugs, or alcohol is a trap to avoid. All three may make you forget about your problems, but they will not help you with your BURNOUT. In fact, they will most likely make your BURNOUT worse.

Lastly, don't try to run away from your problems. Like the saying goes, "When the going gets tough, those suffering from BURNOUT get going — in the other direction." It is so tempting to run away from your problems. You may remember Hagar's solution to her problems, in the book of Genesis, was to run away and leave Ishmael under a bush. God intervened for Hagar, and He will intervene and help you, if you will seek His help.

You can avoid all the above traps, if you remember to get away physically every once in a while. Remember to have a photo or something close to you at work so you can get away mentally every once in a while. Spend time daily in prayer, take time to rest, and remember to exercise. All of these methods of escape will help you recover from your BURNOUT.

Chapter 10

R

R is for remember.

Before my dad passed away, he and my mom got Jerry and me the best Christmas present ever. In the past, they have given us a side of beef, a washing machine, and firewood, but it was not any of those gifts. What could it be, a car, flat screen TV, or a certificate of deposit? No, it was a toilet. But not just any toilet, this thing was scary. If not careful, you could lose your backside or a limb when it flushed. Instead of a ball thingee in the tank on the back of the toilet, it had an air tank. At least now you know why I am a lawyer, and not a plumber. That toilet was awesome.

It is crazy how a toilet can be the best gift, but just think about 100 years ago how true that was. It is so hard to believe that people had no indoor plumbing, and no super soft, aloe scented, 8-ply toilet paper. How did they survive? It is hard to appreciate just how nice indoor plumbing is if you have never had to experience not having it.

That same statement can be made about so many things. You can't appreciate a flat screen TV unless you have had a box TV as big as your living room. Unless you have had to go over and change TV channels by hand, you cannot appreciate a remote control. You can't appreciate a woman's voice on your car's GPS screen telling you which way to go unless you have had your wife's voice telling you where to go. Trust me on this one.

We need to **REMEMBER** just how good we have it. When you are struggling with BURNOUT, you forget about anything good and concentrate on the bad. You think about how bad something that happened was, or how bad you feel, or how bad life is.

It is true, God never promised us a rose garden just as country singer Lynn Anderson sang so well. In fact, in John 16:33, God promises us that we will have troubles in this world. But, in the very same verse, He also tells us not to worry because He has overcome the world.

Life isn't easy and we do have troubles, but all in all, we have it pretty good.

To help recover from BURNOUT, we need to start thinking and remembering how good we have it. Remember all the good things in life. Remember things like ketchup, 5 hour gum, your spouse, airplanes, March Madness basketball, PB&J sandwiches, Brady Bunch reruns, and fruitcake (okay maybe not fruitcake). God has given us so many things that we need to always remember to be thankful.

Have you ever been to church and sang, "Count your many blessings, name them one by one?" That song is ridiculous. I mean..........are you serious? Have you ever tried that? You wouldn't hear the sermon, or go to work the next day, or do anything for a month, if you tried to name them one by one. That's the point. God has blessed us beyond what we deserve, and beyond our wildest imaginations.

Maybe your job is causing your BURNOUT. If so, remember that there are worse jobs in the world. When our son, Alex, was young, he had a book named *Grossology*. In that book, it had a photo of a lady going up to a man's underarm and sniffing. There was a line of men for her to do the same thing. Her job was a deodorant tester. Think about that next time you think you have the worst job in the world. Also, think about the person in the circus whose job it is to follow the elephant around and clean up after him. Is your job that bad?

As a prosecutor, you may not get paid as much as criminal defense attorneys. It makes you start to whine and complain about your job. You start thinking, if I just did one DWI guilty plea per day as a defense attorney, then I could make over $50,000 per year. How easy would that be? You start to regret your job decision.

You forget about what a criminal defense attorney has to deal with on a daily basis. And, you forget that you are helping people. Because of something you did, maybe one less drunk driver is on the road at night. Maybe somebody is alive because of you. Maybe one less sex offender is abusing little kids, because you helped take one off the streets that day in court. A victim might not get beat up tonight because of the difference you made. Does it matter how little money you make if you helped in any of the above situations?

Whatever job you have, you do get paid, right? It was a job you applied for, and you knew going in how much money they would pay you. That always brings me back to my least favorite parable in the Bible. You know the one, in Matthew, Chapter 20, the parable of the workers in the vineyard. In that parable, the worker in the morning gets the same money as the one that is hired later in the day. It doesn't seem fair, does it?

The point of the parable obviously is that none of us deserve the love God has shown us. And, we should not be concerned with what others have, but only with how blessed we are.

When remembering how good we have things, think about this too. The average world-wide income is $7,000. Only about 19% of the world's population lives in a country with incomes that high. As of 2005, people in the so-called rich countries (those above $7,000) only had an average income of $35,000.[5]

If your BURNOUT is from job stress, the above statistics will help you realize that maybe things really are not that bad after all.

But what if your BURNOUT was like mine, from the death of a child or other loved one? How could things be worse? The best answer for that is to look at the example of Job in the Bible. I would say Job had it pretty bad. He lost all his possessions, his servants, his health, and his children, yet still kept his faith in God. Job could have quit on God. Instead, the Bible says that Job "fell to the ground" (Job 1:20) and worshiped God.

Another good example to follow is that of Horatio Spafford. "Who is that?" you might ask. Horatio Spafford was an attorney in Chicago. He lived there during the great fire in 1871. Around that same time, he and his wife lost their son to illness. Their four daughters were still alive. Later their family decided to take a vacation. They were going to England by boat. Horatio had business to attend to and was to follow them in a few days. The boat never made it to England. Although Horatio's wife was able to cling to a piece of wreckage, all of his daughters--Maggie, Tanetta, Annie, and Bessie--were killed. Horatio went to meet his wife, and on the way there wrote one of the best Christian hymns we sing. It is said that he wrote the hymn along the same spot as where his daughters' ship had gone down. The hymn is "It is Well with My Soul." Just absorb the lyrics from one of the verses of that hymn:

> When peace, like a river, attendeth my way,
> When sorrows like sea billows roll;
> Whatever my lot, Thou has taught me to say,
> It is well, it is well, with my soul.

Horatio Spafford was a true man of faith, and an example for all of us who have lost loved ones.

Lastly, look at the story of Joseph in Genesis. I don't know if he was suffering from BURNOUT, but he was down in the pits. Okay, I realize that is a bad joke, but Joseph was thrown in a pit by his brothers. We all know what happened next – God saved Joseph. And actually, saved all the Jews because of Joseph, including Joseph's family. The point is, God is in control. Remember, He has a plan, and someday everything will be revealed and none of us will have any problems or worries, let alone any BURNOUT issues.

Chapter 11

Smooth as Butter

If you have not heard of Bethany Hamilton, I urge you to do a *Google* search and find out more about her. She is the beautiful, brave young girl who was bitten by a shark while surfing in Hawaii. She lost her arm in the attack, but she didn't lose her spirit. Bethany continues to surf, and continues to inspire countless people around the world. On the front page of her website is a verse from Psalms. It is Psalm 103:1-2, "Let all that I am praise the Lord; may I never forget the good things he does for me."

Bethany Hamilton's true story was made into the movie *Soul Surfer*. That movie documents Bethany's struggles, her surfing, her mission trip to Thailand, and her faith. In the final scene of the movie, a news reporter asks the actress that plays Bethany if she had it to do all over again, would she still go surfing that day. The answer was "yes" because her injury gave her the opportunity to embrace more people than she ever could have with two arms, and to be an example for them.

Now, I don't know that I can go that far. I would have prosecuted the defendants for robbing and killing the store clerk, even knowing I might get sued. However, I think I would have kept Ashley at home that day, and maybe every day after

78

that.

It all boils down to the fact that we are given what we are given in life. How we cope with it, and what we do next is all up to us. None of us is given more than we can handle. Life may drag us down, and we may become burned out on everything. All we can do is make the best of things and try and recover.

Have you ever spread butter on toast? It just goes on so smoothly. That is the way I want my life to be .... as smooth as butter. It doesn't always work out that way. I cannot guarantee you that your life or mine will be as smooth as butter, even if you follow my F.I.N.G.E.R. philosophy.

I can guarantee you that F.I.N.G.E.R. has helped and continues to help me in my recovery. I strongly believe that those of us suffering from BURNOUT need to try something. But what if you cannot remember the acronym F.I.N.G.E.R.?

Remember when you were a child and intertwined your fingers together and formed a church and steeple. Yeah, you know what comes next, don't you? Here is the church, here is the steeple, open the doors, and see all the people. Unless you have young children or grandchildren, you probably have not done that in years, but, you remembered exactly how to do it. That is because most of us are visual learners.

The best way I can think of for you to visually learn my F.I.N.G.E.R. philosophy is to think of how it could make your life as smooth as butter. Put those two words together, and you obviously get *Butterfinger*. I suggest you put a *Butterfinger* wrapper on your desk, in your car, at your bedside, or wherever you will notice it the most. Use it as a constant reminder of a way to cope with BURNOUT. You are welcome to leave the candy in the wrapper, but what is the fun in that?!

Start to have **F**un and laughter again in your life. Remember what is **I**mportant: your faith, family and friends. Take some time and look back at **N**otes you have received in the past that make you feel better. **G**ive back in big or small ways, to those around you. Find a way to **E**scape to your happy place, whether physically or just in a daydream. And, always **R**emember how blessed you are.

One of my favorite verses in the Bible is the Message Version of II Corinthians 4:17. There Paul writes, "These hard times are small potatoes compared to the coming good times, the lavish celebration prepared for us."

Always remember that whatever the reason for your BURNOUT, whether loss of a loved one, or job related issues, or being sued for 24 million dollars, or a combination of all of the above, they are all small potatoes compared to how great heaven is going to be. That verse gives me so much comfort, as I hope it does you.

I also hope that this book gives you some measure of comfort and hope. My prayer is that I conveyed the words that

God wanted me to convey, and that this F.I.N.G.E.R. philosophy helps you recover and cope in your daily struggles with your BURNOUT issues.

God bless.

Endnotes:

1. Maslach, C., Jackson, S.E., & Leiter, M.P. *MBI: The Maslach Burnout Inventory: Manual.* Palo Alto: Consulting Psychologists Press, 1996.

2. Kristensen, T.S., Borritz, M., Villadsen, E., & Christensen, K.B. *The Copenhagen Burnout Inventory: A new tool for the assessment of burnout.* Work & Stress, 2005, 19, 192-207.; Shirom, A. & Melamed, S. *Does burnout affect physical health? A review of the evidence.* In A.S.G. Antoniou & C. L. Cooper (Eds.), Research companion to organizational health psychology (pp. 599-622). Cheltenham, UK: Edward Elgar, 2005.

3. The Ohio State University Department of Aging, *Identifying the Difference between Stress and Burnout.* (2007)

4. Lawyers with Depression, *Depression Statistics in General and in Lawyers*, 2011.

5. The Globalist, *The Globalist Quiz: Average Earnings Worldwide*, 2007.